Junior Drug Awareness

Nicotine & Cigarettes

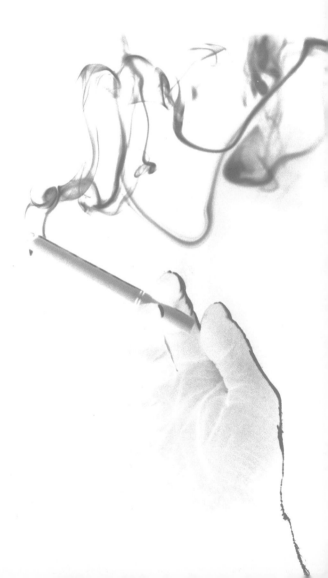

Junior Drug Awareness

Alcohol

Amphetamines and Other Uppers

Crack and Cocaine

Ecstasy and Other Designer Drugs

Heroin

How to Get Help

How to Say No

Inhalants and Solvents

LSD, PCP, and Other Hallucinogens

Marijuana

Nicotine and Cigarettes

Pain Relievers, Diet Pills, and
   Other Over-the-Counter Drugs

Prozac and Other Antidepressants

Steroids

Valium and Other Downers

Junior Drug Awareness

Nicotine & Cigarettes

Introduction by **BARRY R. McCAFFREY**
Director, Office of National Drug Control Policy

Foreword by **STEVEN L. JAFFE, M.D.**
Senior Consulting Editor,
Professor of Child and Adolescent Psychiatry, Emory University

Gina De Angelis

Chelsea House Publishers
Philadelphia

The author wishes to dedicate this book to all of her family members (smokers and non-smokers) who have died of cancer and other lung diseases.

CHELSEA HOUSE PUBLISHERS
Editor in Chief Stephen Reginald
Production Manager Pamela Loos
Director of Photography Judy L. Hasday
Art Director Sara Davis
Managing Editor James D. Gallagher
Senior Production Editor LeeAnne Gelletly

Staff for NICOTINE & CIGARETTES
Project Editor Therese De Angelis
Senior Editor John Ziff
Editorial Assistant Jessica Carey
Associate Art Director Takeshi Takahashi
Picture Researcher Sandy Jones
Designer Keith Trego
Cover Illustrator/Designer Takeshi Takahashi

Cover photo © Telegraph Colour Library/
            FPG International

The Chelsea House World Wide Web site address is http://www.chelseahouse.com

First Printing
1 3 5 7 9 8 6 4 2

Library of Congress Cataloging-in-Publication Data
Applied for
ISBN 0-7910-5175-7

CONTENTS

by Barry R. McCaffrey
Director, Office of National
Drug Control Policy

STAYING AWAY FROM ILLEGAL DRUGS, TOBACCO PRODUCTS, AND ALCOHOL

G ood health allows you to be as strong, happy, smart, and skillful as you can possibly be. The worst thing about illegal drugs is that they damage people from the inside. Our bodies and minds are wonderful, complicated systems that run like finely tuned machines when we take care of ourselves.

Doctors prescribe legal drugs, called medicines, to heal us when we become sick, but dangerous chemicals that are not recommended by doctors, nurses, or pharmacists are called illegal drugs. These drugs cannot be bought in stores because they harm different organs of the body, causing illness or even death. Illegal drugs, such as marijuana, cocaine or "crack," heroin, methamphetamine ("meth"), and other dangerous substances are against the law because they affect our ability to think, work, play, sleep, or eat.

If anyone ever offers you illegal drugs or any kind of pills, liquids, substances to smoke, or shots to inject into your body, tell them you're not interested. You should report drug pushers—people who distribute these poisons—to parents, teachers, police, coaches, clergy, or other adults whom you trust.

Cigarettes and alcohol are also illegal for youngsters. Tobacco products and drinks like wine, beer, and liquor are particularly harmful for children and teenagers because their bodies, especially their nervous systems, are still developing. For this reason, young people are more likely to be hurt by illicit drugs—including cigarettes and alcohol. These two products kill more people—from cancer, and automobile accidents caused by intoxicated drivers—than all other drugs combined. We say about drug use: "Users are losers." Be a winner and stay away from illegal drugs, tobacco products, and alcoholic beverages.

Here are four reasons why you shouldn't use illegal drugs:

- Illegal drugs can cause brain damage.
- Illegal drugs are "psychoactive." This means that they change your personality or the way you feel. They also impair your judgment. While under the influence of drugs, you are more likely to endanger your life or someone else's. You will also be less able to protect yourself from danger.
- Many illegal drugs are addictive, which means that once a person starts taking them, stopping is extremely difficult. An addict's body craves the drug and becomes dependent upon it. The illegal drug–user may become sick if the drug is discontinued and so may become a slave to drugs.

- Some drugs, called "gateway" substances, can lead a person to take more-dangerous drugs. For example, a 12-year-old who smokes marijuana is 79 times more likely to have an addiction problem later in life than a child who never tries marijuana.

Here are some reasons why you shouldn't drink alcoholic beverages, including beer and wine coolers:

- Alcohol is the second leading cause of death in our country. More than 100,000 people die every year because of drinking.
- Adolescents are twice as likely as adults to be involved in fatal alcohol-related car crashes.
- Half of all assaults against girls or women involve alcohol.
- Drinking is illegal if you are under the age of 21. You could be arrested for this crime.

Here are three reasons why you shouldn't smoke cigarettes:

- Nicotine is highly addictive. Once you start smoking, it is very hard to stop, and smoking cigarettes causes lung cancer and other diseases. Tobacco- and nicotine-related diseases kill more than 400,000 people every year.
- Each day, 3,000 kids begin smoking. One-third of these youngsters will probably have their lives shortened because of tobacco use.
- Children who smoke cigarettes are almost six times more likely to use other illegal drugs than kids who don't smoke.

If your parents haven't told you how they feel about the dangers of illegal drugs, ask them. One of every 10 kids aged 12 to 17 is using illegal drugs. They do not understand the risks they are taking with their health and their lives. However, the vast majority of young people in America are smart enough to figure out that drugs, cigarettes, and alcohol could rob them of their future. Be your body's best friend: guard your mental and physical health by staying away from drugs.

WHY SHOULD I LEARN ABOUT DRUGS?

Steven L. Jaffe, M.D., Senior Consulting Editor,
Professor of Child and Adolescent Psychiatry,
Emory University

Your grandparents and great-grandparents did not think much about "drug awareness." That's because drugs, to most of them, simply meant "medicine."

Of the three types of drugs, medicine is the good type. Medicines such as penicillin and aspirin promote healing and help sick people get better.

Another type of drug is obviously bad for you because it is poison. Then there are the kinds of drugs that fool you, such as marijuana and LSD. They make you feel good, but they harm your body and brain.

Our great crisis today is that this third category of drugs has become widely abused. Drugs of abuse are everywhere, not just in rough neighborhoods. Many teens are introduced to drugs by older brothers, sisters, friends, or even friends' parents. Some people may use only a little bit of a drug, but others who inherited a tendency to become addicted may move on to using drugs all the time. If a family member is or was an alcoholic or an addict, a young person is at greater risk of becoming one.

Drug abuse can weaken us physically. Worse, it can cause permanent mental damage. Our brain is the most important part of our body. Our thoughts, hopes, wishes, feelings, and memories are located there, within 100 billion nerve cells. Alcohol and drugs that are abused will harm—and even destroy—these cells. During the teen years, your brain continues to develop and grow, but drugs and alcohol can impair this growth.

I treat all types of teenagers at my hospital programs and in my office. Many suffer from depression or anxiety. A lot of them abuse drugs and alcohol, and this makes their depression or fears worse. I have celebrated birthdays and high school graduations with many of my patients. But I have also been to sad funerals for others who have died from problems with drug abuse.

Doctors understand more about drugs today than ever before. We've learned that some substances (even some foods) that we once thought were harmless can actually cause health problems. And for some people, medicines that help relieve one symptom might cause problems in other ways. This is because each person's body chemistry and immune system are different.

For all of these reasons, drug awareness is important for everyone. We need to learn which drugs to avoid or question—not only the destructive, illegal drugs we hear so much about in the news, but also ordinary medicines we buy at the supermarket or pharmacy. We need to understand that even "good" drugs can hurt us if they are not used correctly. We also need accurate scientific knowledge, not just rumors we hear from other teens.

Drug awareness enables you to make good decisions. It allows you to become powerful and strong and have a meaningful life!

Do you smoke? Do you think you can quit after trying "just a few" cigarettes? You may be dead wrong. Read this chapter to find out what can happen after you smoke just one cigarette.

A COMMON DRUG

Did you know that **nicotine** is a highly poisonous chemical? In quantities smaller than a drop (70 milligrams), it can cause tremors, nausea, and vomiting. It can even cause immediate death by slowing down the body's central nervous system (made up of the brain and spinal cord).

Is this the same chemical that is found in cigarettes? Yes, it is! But the reason smoking a cigarette doesn't kill a smoker immediately is that a cigarette contains only a very small amount—about 0.5 to 2 milligrams—of nicotine. Even in small amounts, though, nicotine is an extremely dangerous drug that can cause **addiction**. Some studies even suggest that nicotine is as addictive as illegal drugs like **heroin** and **cocaine**.

Cigarettes are not the only tobacco products that contain nicotine. Cigars, pipe tobacco, **snuff** or **dip**, **chewing tobacco**, and **bidis** (pronounced "bee-deez") are other tobacco products that contain this chemical. The risks to a user's health vary depending on the type of tobacco and how it is taken (smoked, chewed, or snorted). But all of them have one thing in common: nicotine.

Tobacco and Addiction

As you might have guessed, the most popular kind of tobacco product is cigarettes—dried, shredded tobacco leaves rolled in thin paper, often with a small filter attached. When the user inhales the smoke from the burning tobacco, nicotine immediately enters the lungs and quickly reaches the brain. It takes only about eight seconds for nicotine in a cigarette to reach the brain. That's faster than the time it takes for injected heroin or cocaine, which is about 12 seconds!

Cigars are pieces of tobacco leaves rolled whole, with no filter. Cigar users do not usually inhale the smoke from a cigar; instead, they hold it in their mouths and absorb the nicotine that way. Pipe tobacco is shredded tobacco that is specially treated and flavored to be burned in a pipe. Depending on the blend of tobacco used, the nicotine from pipe tobacco is absorbed either through the membranes of the mouth or through the lungs.

Snuff, which in its dry form was very popular in the 18th century, is powdered tobacco that is inhaled through the nose. "Moist snuff" is the most popular kind of snuff in the United States. Also called **spit tobacco** or "dip," it is held in the mouth, either loose or wrapped in a small packet. It is not chewed.

Chewing tobacco is chewed or held in the mouth for

Every day, 3,000 kids begin smoking. One of the reasons these kids give for starting to use tobacco is peer pressure: they feel that they need to do what their friends are doing to fit in with the crowd. Despite what you may think, however, "everyone" doesn't smoke, and you don't have to do what others do to fit in.

long periods of time. It is available as loose leaves, "plugs" (small cakes), or twists, and like snuff it often contains added flavors.

A new and dangerous fad among young people is the practice of smoking **bidis**—thin, unfiltered cigarettes imported from India. Bidis have become popular because they are cheaper than American cigarettes and come in several flavors, such as chocolate, cherry, and cinnamon. Many kids think that bidis are "safer" than standard cigarettes, but they are wrong: bidis deliver *twice* the amount of **tar** and *seven times* the amount of nicotine of regular cigarettes. And in many cases, packages of bidis do not carry warnings about the hazards of smoking. See page 17 for more information about bidis.

Like bidis, smokeless tobacco products—snuff and chewing tobacco—are sometimes believed to be safer than cigarettes, but they are not. All tobacco contains nicotine, the addictive agent, and smokeless tobacco often contains much higher levels of nicotine than cigarettes do. In addition, in as little as three years, users can develop **oral cancer** (**cancer** of the mouth, lips, gums, tongue, larynx or voice box, and esophagus, the tube that connects the mouth to the stomach).

If Tobacco Is So Dangerous, Why Do People Use It?

There are many reasons why people start using tobacco, but the most common reason why they keep using it is that they have become **physically dependent** on the nicotine, which means they have become addicted. As with any addictive substance, a user's body adapts to the drug and eventually requires it to function normally. The person develops a **tolerance** to the drug, meaning that he or she requires increasing amounts of the drug to reach the same level of "high" once felt with a smaller amount. Tobacco users will find that they need nicotine just to feel "right" or "normal." If users do not get regular doses of the drug, **withdrawal** symptoms occur.

Some of the symptoms of nicotine withdrawal are drowsiness, irritability, anger, insomnia, dry mouth, indigestion, headache, hunger, constipation, giddiness,

Bidis: A Deadly Fad

A new type of cigarette is becoming a favorite among young adults—even those who do not smoke standard cigarettes. Bidis, which are legally imported from India, are thin, unfiltered cigarettes that are hand-wrapped in brown leaves and tied with short pieces of thread.

Bidis have become popular among school kids under 18—who by law are not permitted to smoke or buy cigarettes—because they look cool, cost less than regular cigarettes, and come in a wide variety of flavors, such as root beer, orange, lemon-lime, almond, clove, and strawberry.

Sound appealing? Then consider this: one bidi contains up to *seven times* more nicotine than a regular filtered cigarette, according to the Centers for Disease Control and Prevention. And even though the tar level of a bidi is about the same as that of standard cigarettes, a bidi smoker inhales more tar because bidis are unfiltered. Even worse, a San Francisco survey found that 70 percent of bidis sold in the United States do not carry the Surgeon General's warning about the health risks of smoking.

Unfortunately, 44 percent of kids who smoke bidis do so because they believe that bidis are not addictive and are less dangerous to one's health than regular cigarettes. They're dead wrong. Like any other tobacco product, bidis can cause cancer and lead to heart disease, high blood pressure, and a host of other serious health problems. They are far more addictive than regular cigarettes.

In 1998, the San Francisco Anti-Smoking Project funded a study of bidi use in the United States. A spokesperson for the project said that about half of bidi users were younger than 18 and thought that bidis were "not really cigarettes."

Now you know better. Bidis *are* cigarettes, and cigarette smoking can kill you.

nausea, weight gain, fatigue, difficulty concentrating, and depression. The most noticeable withdrawal symptom of tobacco is a powerful craving for nicotine. Another effect of quitting tobacco use—particularly smoking—is the urge to do something with one's hands, to go through the familiar and soothing motions of smoking.

Taken individually, these symptoms may not sound very severe, but when many of them are present at one time, a person trying to stop using tobacco may find it much easier to take up his or her habit again rather than "tough it out" and stay tobacco-free. (Some products, such as **nicotine gum**, deliver small amounts of nicotine without the harmful effects of tobacco, thus helping people quit.)

But as you can imagine, there are many good reasons to quit. More than 400,000 Americans die prematurely every year from diseases caused by cigarette smoking. This is greater than the number of deaths from AIDS, alcohol abuse, car accidents, murders, suicides, fires, and all other drugs combined.

So Why Do People Start Smoking?

That's a good question! Most of the people who begin smoking are teenagers—and some are even younger. Every day in the United States, 3,000 children start smoking. Many of these children probably once promised someone they loved that they would never smoke. Why do they start?

Young smokers often believe that only a *lifetime* of

tobacco use is dangerous. Studies show, however, that an addiction to nicotine is stronger in those who begin smoking at a younger age. Most teens who smoke say they probably will not be smoking after high school, but statistics show that the majority still smoke between seven and nine years later. More than 90 percent of adult smokers started when they were teens. They didn't think they'd get addicted either. Addiction to nicotine, just like addiction to other drugs, can start the first time a person tries the drug.

So in spite of how temporary your smoking habit might seem, the chances are good that if you are smoking cigarettes at age 12, or even age 9, you'll probably still be smoking when you are 17, 27, or even 77—if you live that long. And if you begin smoking cigarettes, you are more likely to experiment with other drugs, opening the "gateway" to multiple addictions. This is why tobacco, alcohol, and **marijuana** are often referred to as **gateway drugs**.

The cigarette and tobacco habit is second only to alcohol in popularity among teenagers. Tobacco stimu-

Think It's Cool to Smoke? Think Again

Statistics show that teens who smoke have a few things in common: usually they are not involved in school activities, such as drama clubs or sports teams. A majority of them don't like school very much and don't get good grades: one recent study showed that only 7 percent of high school seniors who had an A average smoked, while 46 of those with a D average smoked. And most teens surveyed said they would prefer to date nonsmokers.

lates the nervous system in the same way that cocaine does, and it can be just as addictive. Chewing tobacco is just as bad for your health as smoking it, and as a habit it is equally repulsive. Picture one or two people you know who smoke cigarettes or chew tobacco: do they look cool or silly with those things in their mouths or spitting tobacco juice into an empty can?

One of the main reasons kids begin smoking is **peer pressure**—a term used to describe the influence of your friends and others of your age group. A person whose friends smoke is much more likely to try smoking. So is a person who has older siblings or a parent who smokes. In some cases this is because the person looks up to his or her family members or friends and wants to be like them. Sometimes young people smoke to fit in with "the crowd," or they feel pressured into trying smoking. Feeling left out or being teased for refusing to do something are often strong motivators.

When asked, some teens say that smoking makes them more popular or helps them keep their weight down. Others say it's just something to do when they're bored, or that it makes them feel better when they're under stress. Others say they're just "experimenting." But again, statistics show that teens who smoke have some things in common: they usually aren't involved in school activities, such as clubs or sports teams. They usually don't like school in general and don't get good grades. And if they think smoking makes them more popular, they're probably wrong: most teens say they'd like to date nonsmokers.

Tobacco-related disease is the number-one preventable cause of death in the United States. It's important for young people to know why tobacco is so dangerous, and to find ways to say no to using it. In the next chapter, we'll explore the history of tobacco and find out how using it became so popular.

A farmer harvests tobacco plants in southwestern China. Most of the world's tobacco is grown, processed, and used in China. The United States—particularly the South—is also an important source of tobacco. Cultivators of small farms find tobacco an appealing crop because they earn more money growing it than they would growing crops such as corn, rice, or wheat.

TOBACCO'S LONG HISTORY

The species of plant known as *Nicotiana tabacum* is one of the most dangerous plants in the world. Tobacco originated in South America and spread to North America many centuries ago. Until Christopher Columbus reached the New World, Europeans had never heard of "drinking smoke," as they called it.

About two thousand years ago, South American cultures began using tobacco. Brazilian peoples invented cigarettes by rolling tobacco leaves in paper. In Central America and what is now Mexico, the Mayan and Aztec peoples smoked tobacco leaves in hollow plant stems. Farther north, Native Americans used tobacco in pipes for religious and other ceremonies. They believed it could provide protection and even magical powers—the plant was thought to be a gift from the Great Spirit. Tobacco use spread to the West Indies, where Columbus landed, and the 15th-century explorer himself brought tobacco back to Europe with him.

Not surprisingly, the first Europeans to use tobacco regularly were sailors. Wherever they traveled, they brought tobacco with them and encouraged people to grow it so that the next time the sailors visited that port they would be able to buy tobacco there. By about 1575, according to one account, tobacco use had spread to every nation in the world.

The Cure-All Drug

At first, many people believed that tobacco cured a number of illnesses. It was called an *herba panacea*—a cure-all herb. People were told that it could cure fevers, toothaches, or nausea, or even the dreaded disease known as the Black Death (**bubonic plague**). Famous figures such as Sir Walter Raleigh made smoking fashionable among the wealthy elite. (The first time a servant saw Raleigh smoking, he thought his master was on fire and dumped a bucket of water on his head!) Some people even believed that smoking cleaned out the lungs.

At first, few people agreed with the English king James I, who believed that smoking was "a custom lothsome to the eye, hatefull to the Nose, harmeful to the braine, dangerous to the Lungs, and in the blacke stinking fume thereof, neerest resembling the horrible Stigian [hellish] smoke of the pit that is bottomlesse." Instead, most people believed tobacco had medicinal value. Jean Nicot, a French ambassador, sent tobacco plants home

This medicine bundle belonged to a member of a "tobacco society" of the Crow, a Native American tribe of the Great Plains. Many Native American tribes believed tobacco was a sacred plant, and they used it during religious healing ceremonies to cure specific ailments, such as earaches, burns and scalds, stomach cramps, and skin inflammations.

from his post in Portugal in 1559, telling friends it was useful for treating wounds, **asthma**, and cancer. (The words *nicotine* and *nicotiana* come from Jean Nicot's last name. The actual chemical was first isolated by French scientists in 1828.)

Beginning in the 1920s in America, it became socially acceptable for women to smoke. This measure of equality has produced unfortunate results: the American Lung Association estimated that 67,000 women died of smoking-related lung cancer in 1998.

A Deadly Poison

Tobacco is a poisonous plant: the poison in it is nicotine. Tobacco plants contain nicotine as a natural defense, to keep bugs from eating their leaves. At one time nicotine was used in some **pesticides**, but because it is such a strong poison, that use is no longer allowed. Workers on tobacco farms sometimes suffer nicotine poisoning when they absorb the chemical through their skin. And babies and young children have been poisoned by sucking on tobacco leaves or eating cigarettes. Even the small amount of nicotine in tobacco smoke has a very powerful effect on those who abuse the drug—and anyone who uses tobacco is abusing nicotine.

Several countries outlawed tobacco use in the 1600s. In Turkey during that period, tobacco users could be tortured or killed. In China, a person caught with tobacco might be beheaded. In Russia, tobacco users who were caught a second time were killed.

By about 1700, chemists and scholars had recognized some of the harmful effects of tobacco and no longer thought its use healthful. By the end of the 1700s most other people agreed. But by then, thousands, if not millions, of people were addicted to the nicotine in tobacco, and using tobacco was still fashionable. For Spain and the American colonies especially, tobacco was extremely important to the economy. It had become a major crop, and it provided income for many people. For a while in the American colonies, tobacco was so valuable that it could be used in place of money. People in early Virginia planted it in every square of soil they could find. In fact, the Virginia Company, which sponsored the early colony, had to pass a law requiring people to grow food also, and not just tobacco.

Like King James I, who put a 4,000 percent tax on tobacco, many national leaders eventually decided to tax tobacco as a way to try stamping out its use while making money for their governments. In many cases, however, these taxes only made governments dependent on the tax money. In countries where tobacco was heavily taxed and not readily available, people began smuggling tobacco to avoid paying the taxes. Today, a number of world governments still make billions of dollars in revenue from the taxes collected from tobacco users. And in some countries, many people still use the **black market** (a system of producing, distributing, or selling a product illegally) to get tobacco products or to avoid paying taxes on them. Like alcohol, tobacco is both pleasure-inducing and very harmful—and attempts to stamp it out using taxes and laws have generally failed.

Smoking, Chewing, and Snorting

As popular and government reactions to tobacco changed over time, so did ways of using tobacco. Until the 1700s, pipe smoking was the preferred method of tobacco use. Then some people began to use dry snuff or chewing tobacco instead. By the 1800s, cigarettes became more fashionable, but they had to be rolled by hand and were very expensive.

Tobacco use increased in America during and after the Civil War because machines of the mid– and late 1800s made cigarettes cheap and plentiful. In the early 20th century, use of the safety match—one that can be struck and ignited only on a specially prepared friction surface—allowed people to smoke virtually anywhere, not just near a source of flame. Cigars and chewing tobacco were still more popular than cigarettes, but during and after World War I, cigarettes caught up and eventually became the dominant tobacco product.

Cigarette companies often try to portray smoking as sophisticated and glamorous, but what you don't see in such advertisements are the deadly effects of smoking.

A Banned Substance?

At the same time, scientists were beginning to examine the health effects of using tobacco. The first report to link smoking to certain diseases was published in 1859. Around the same time, the possibility that tobacco created a physical dependence was also under investigation. By the late 1800s, several influential people declared that tobacco use should be banned; among them were the inventor Thomas Edison and the automobile maker Henry Ford. Another reformer was Lucy

Page Gaston, a schoolteacher who, along with other activists, helped pass laws that prevented the sale of tobacco to minors. By 1890, 26 U.S. states had such laws. In 1899 Gaston founded the Chicago Anti-Cigarette League.

After World War I, a group of tobacco companies joined together and denied that tobacco causes any harmful effects. (Until recently these companies continued to stand by that denial, even though they knew it to be false.) Instead of admitting that their product caused serious health problems, the tobacco industry used clever advertising and marketing techniques to encourage people to smoke. They tried to make smoking look safe. Movie stars, athletes, and even doctors and nurses appeared in cigarette advertisements, endorsing the use of tobacco. The Tobacco Merchants Association funded **lobbyists** in Washington, D.C., and in state capitals. Lobbyists are people who try to influence lawmakers to pass laws that will benefit their cause, or not to pass laws that will harm their cause. By 1927 they had succeeded in reversing all laws banning cigarettes.

During World War I and World War II, soldiers were given cigarettes as part of their rations. Millions of men came home from these wars addicted to tobacco. After World War II, cigarette sales were higher than ever. And, beginning in the 1920s, it became more and more socially acceptable for women to smoke. The health consequences for women have been severe: in 1985, lung cancer surpassed breast cancer as the leading killer of American women.

In other parts of the world, tobacco production increased in the last half of the 20th century. Today, the biggest percentage of the world's tobacco is grown in China, although other places in Asia and the Americas are also big producers. Some of these countries don't export very much tobacco—most of China's tobacco is used in China, for example. Other important tobacco-producing countries include India, Brazil, Turkey, Zimbabwe, Russia, and of course, the United States (particularly the southern states).

The Money-Making Plant

Usually, small farmers decide to grow tobacco because they can make much more money selling it than they could selling corn, rice, or other food products. One acre of a tobacco crop can be worth $3,862— more than five times the value of an acre of peanuts! By contrast, a cotton farmer might earn $380 an acre for his or her crop, and a wheat farmer a comparatively tiny $100 an acre.

But tobacco also costs a lot of money to raise, and it wears out the soil, so that more fertilizers and chemicals are needed to grow it. Tobacco companies and governments **subsidize** many farmers who want to start growing tobacco, particularly in Africa and other developing areas.

Tobacco is a labor-intensive crop, meaning that it takes more work to produce a certain amount of ready-to-sell tobacco than it does to produce, for example, the same amount of tomatoes. First, the plants have to be

Did you know that nicotine is a poison that the tobacco plant uses to protect itself? Because tobacco is usually harvested by hand, workers must be careful to avoid being poisoned.

grown in a greenhouse and carefully tended. Only certain kinds of tobacco can be grown in certain regions. Then the ground must be prepared, so that insects and germs won't kill the tobacco plants. This requires burning the ground or putting chemicals into the earth. The plants will later absorb some of these chemicals.

Next, the plants have to be transplanted to the fields. The ground has to be damp and the weather has to be warm. The plants must be watered if there isn't enough rain. They are constantly checked in case mold develops, or weeds or insects threaten the crop. They are continually fertilized because the plants drain so many nutrients from the earth. When it's time to harvest the plants, many seasonal workers are called in to gather them by hand so the leaves aren't damaged. The weather must be dry for the harvest. Pickers must be very careful to avoid nicotine poisoning from the plants.

After the harvest, the leaves undergo **curing**. This involves drying the leaves partially but not completely. "The curing process is a difficult one," says author Philip Cohen in his book *Tobacco*, "requiring several days of careful temperature control and constant tending." If the curing is not completed properly, the whole crop may be lost. The companies that subsidize some farmers also send employees to the farms to teach the farmers how to raise and cure tobacco.

Curing is done in barns or large sheds. The leaves are hung up so that air circulates among them, and sometimes they are steamed to retain their moisture. In some curing sheds, electric fans blow warm air through the leaves. The warm air is produced in a furnace outside the shed. This uses up a great deal of wood for fuel. In other curing barns the walls are screened or covered with netting so that breezes blow through. In still other places, the leaves are left out to dry in the sun for a few weeks.

Once the leaves are cured, they are packed and shipped, either to a factory or to an auction where the bundles are sold. In some places the tobacco crop is paid for before it has even finished growing. In the United States, tobacco is sold at auctions.

The Bureau of Alcohol, Tobacco and Firearms (ATF) is a federal agency that oversees tobacco processing plants in the United States. The processing plants make the tobacco into cigarettes, cigars, snuff, chewing tobacco, and pipe tobacco. In the factories, the tobacco is treated with many different chemicals: flavorings, sugars, syrups, licorice, and other substances that affect the taste and other qualities. For example, some chemicals added to the tobacco make it burn more steadily.

Many small farmers in developing countries like to grow tobacco for the money they make in the short term. However, some of them end up having little land left to grow food for their families, and they must borrow money from tobacco companies or from the government to harvest the crop. Then they have to pay back the loans with the money from the crop. The short-term income may be good for these farmers, but in the long run, raising tobacco is risky.

Tobacco farming is devastating to the environment. The plants wear out the soil and spoil the land for other crops. They also take up a great deal of moisture from the soil, causing water tables and underground water (wells) to dry up. Curing tobacco requires huge quantities of wood. In some parts of the world, entire forests have disappeared after only a few years of nearby tobacco farming. The trees are rarely replanted, and since tobacco grows best in semi-arid areas, deserts are spreading because of tobacco farming.

Scientists and doctors have long studied the effects of tobacco use. But after several hundred years, researchers are still just beginning to see how dangerous tobacco is. In 1988, the Surgeon General of the United States declared that nicotine is as addictive as cocaine or heroin. The next chapter will explain some of the risks to your brain and body from using tobacco in any form.

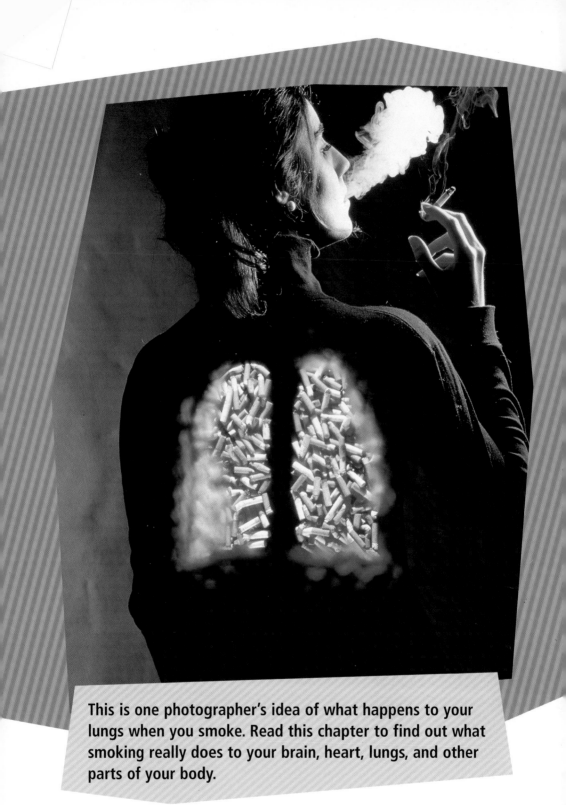

This is one photographer's idea of what happens to your lungs when you smoke. Read this chapter to find out what smoking really does to your brain, heart, lungs, and other parts of your body.

3

WHAT NICOTINE AND SMOKING DO TO YOUR BODY

The first time a person smokes, he or she usually thinks it's pretty gross! Smoking makes you cough and wheeze, and it may make you feel nauseated and dizzy. Your heart rate increases by 15 to 25 beats per minute. Your skin temperature drops six degrees, your blood sugar level decreases, and your appetite is suppressed by nicotine's effect on the **hypothalamus** (a gland in the brain that controls your appetite and moods).

After a while, though, smoking becomes more pleasurable. Smokers eventually develop a tolerance to nicotine: they must use more and more tobacco to get the same feelings of pleasure they once got with a smaller amount. About half of the nicotine from a cigarette is broken down in the body within 20 to 30 minutes. This means that after that amount of time, the smoker will crave nicotine again.

Nicotine and Your Brain

When tobacco is smoked, it takes only eight seconds for nicotine to go from the lungs to the brain. Nicotine is a **stimulant**, meaning that it speeds up the body's activities, particularly in the brain, heart, and nervous system (other stimulants are caffeine, cocaine, and amphetamines). Like other stimulants, it constricts (tightens) the blood vessels, forcing the heart to work harder to pump the same amount of blood through the circulatory system. This raises the body's **blood pressure**. But now the blood has less oxygen in it, and without enough oxygen, brain cells die.

These physical changes cause some people to feel energized or more awake after smoking a cigarette or using tobacco. Others feel more relaxed and calm. A low blood level of nicotine acts as a stimulant, making a person feel more alert, but a greater amount in the bloodstream acts as a tranquilizer, making a person feel relaxed.

Inhaling Poisons

The tip of a cigarette can reach 2,000 degrees Fahrenheit. This makes the cigarette a miniature blast furnace! And the smoker is inhaling the exhaust from that furnace. Although almost all of the thousands of chemicals in tobacco are dangerous (at least 40 of them are known to cause cancer), burning tobacco creates two substances that are particularly harmful: tar and carbon monoxide.

Tar is present in very small particles in cigarette smoke, but when the smoke cools, the tar solidifies in the lungs into a sticky brown or black mass. Tar causes many kinds of cancer and lung diseases such as **emphysema** and chronic **bronchitis**. A smoker is 10 to 30 times more likely than a nonsmoker to develop lung cancer.

Carbon monoxide is a colorless and odorless gas produced when organic materials are burned where there is little oxygen—for example, when gasoline is burned in a car engine or tobacco is burned in a cigarette. Carbon monoxide is deadly. When you breathe, **hemoglobin** in your red blood cells carries the oxygen from the air to all parts of your body. But carbon monoxide has a much greater ability to bond with hemoglobin than oxygen does, so when a smoker inhales carbon monoxide, it is this chemical and not oxygen that travels to the brain.

Not getting enough oxygen makes your heart work harder than it has to. As a result, smoking can cause heart disease, high blood pressure, and strokes. Smokers are two to three times more likely than nonsmokers to develop heart disease.

Pipe and cigar smokers also receive tar and carbon monoxide, but usually in lower levels than do cigarette smokers. This is because pipe and cigar smokers usually don't inhale smoke. Nevertheless, the smoke that goes directly into the air from the burning tip of a cigar, cigarette, or pipe is very harmful too. Pipe and cigar smoking have also been linked to mouth and throat cancer as well as other illnesses. And as you now know, pipe tobacco and cigars also contain nicotine, the addictive chemical in all tobacco products.

Smoke in the Air: Nonsmokers at Risk

The person who is smoking is not the only one affected by cigarette, cigar, and pipe smoke. Environmental tobacco smoke, also called **ETS**, affects anyone around a person who smokes tobacco. **Secondhand smoke** and **sidestream smoke** are types of ETS. And **passive smoking**, which occurs when nonsmokers inhale the smoke from nearby burning tobacco, is harmful to everyone, but is especially bad for pregnant women, babies, young children, and the elderly.

Secondhand smoke is what is exhaled after a smoker takes a drag (a deep breath) from a cigarette, cigar, or pipe. With cigarettes, the smoker's lungs filter some of the chemicals and tar from the smoke before it is exhaled. But exhaled smoke still contains **carcinogenic** (cancer-causing) chemicals and many other impurities. And because smokers of pipes and cigars usually don't inhale the smoke into their lungs, the exhaled smoke contains more chemicals and tar. As a result, people around these smokers often have no choice about whether to breathe in those dangerous chemicals.

Sidestream smoke is what comes directly from the tip of the cigarette or cigar or from the pipe itself. Because it has not been filtered, it is far more dangerous than secondhand smoke. This smoke comes directly from the "blast furnace" that is the burning part of the tobacco, so there is much more unburned tar and other harmful

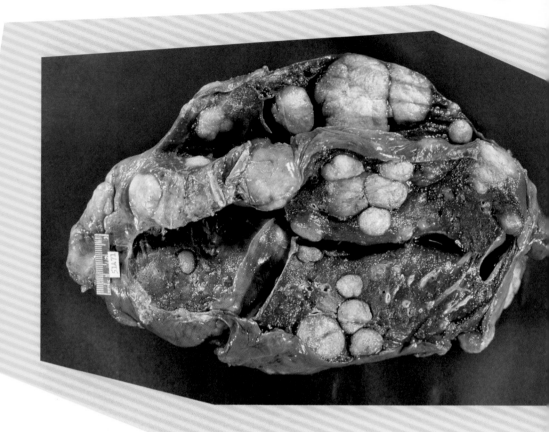

Can you imagine having this inside your body? This is the lung of a person who died from smoking-related lung cancer. Like many teens today, the person probably started out having "just a few cigarettes," and intended to quit soon after starting.

particles in it. Many of these chemicals aren't present in the tobacco itself; they are produced only by burning.

Nonsmokers who are around smokers—for example, a waitress who doesn't smoke but works in a bar, or a child whose parent smokes—have a much greater likelihood than unexposed nonsmokers of contracting illnesses or ailments such as bronchitis, asthma, impaired

People who smoke aren't the only ones who suffer from tobacco-related illnesses. Even nonsmokers can inhale sidestream or second-hand smoke if they are around someone who smokes. Most of us can either leave the area or ask a nearby smoker to put out the cigarette—but the youngster in this photo doesn't have those choices.

breathing, and deadly diseases such as cancer and heart disease. Because it takes many years to develop these diseases, some nonsmokers don't realize the health risks they're exposed to. But passive smoking is still very dangerous. If a nonsmoker lives or works with a smoker, for example, that nonsmoker actually breathes in smoke that is the equivalent of several cigarettes a day. People who live or work around smokers can be up to twice as likely to get sick as unexposed people.

Now that scientists have conducted more studies

involving ETS, news of its risks is getting out. More and more people are becoming aware of the health risks involved not only in smoking itself, but in being around a smoker. In some divorce courts, judges are more likely to award custody of children to the nonsmoking parent than to the smoking parent. Losing custody of a child is a pretty high price to pay for being a smoker.

Smoking and Pregnancy

Even if a woman is not pregnant, the health risks of smoking are no less than those of male smokers, and may even be higher. Women smokers tend to smoke more than men smokers, for example. Smoking more than half a pack (10 cigarettes) a day may cause infertility or irregular menstrual cycles in women. And menopause often occurs earlier in women who smoke than in women who do not.

But for pregnant women, the risks associated with smoking affect another person too. Pregnant women pass any chemicals they take in (from food, tobacco, alcohol, and so on) to their unborn children through the **placenta**. A woman who smokes while she is pregnant can slow down the baby's growth by reducing the amount of oxygen and increasing the amount of carbon monoxide that the baby receives during a critical time when its brain and nervous system are developing.

Babies born of mothers who smoke frequently during pregnancy are on the average seven ounces lighter than other babies. They may also have smaller heads (the head is one-quarter of a baby's birth weight). Birth weight is an indicator of overall health for newborns. "Starting life with below-normal weight," says author Laurence Pringle in *Smoking: A Risky Business*, "a baby born to a smoker is more likely to die in infancy than one born to a nonsmoker."

Smoking while pregnant also increases the chances of spontaneous abortions (miscarriages), stillbirths, and premature labor. Women who smoke have higher risks of giving birth to babies with birth defects or abnormalities. Smoking women may go into labor too soon or have a more difficult time giving birth. And the baby can suffer from complications too. Both the smoking mother and her child are at risk for up to one year after birth. For example, if a smoking mother nurses her child, her baby is still receiving nicotine and other chemicals through her breast milk.

Babies born to women who smoke during pregnancy also grow more slowly than those born to nonsmokers. These children also have a greater risk of dying from SIDS (sudden infant death syndrome), of suffering from hyperactivity, and of being a few months behind their classmates in certain learning skills. Some experts also believe that the child of a woman who smokes while pregnant may have a tougher time staying away from tobacco later in life, because the child developed a tolerance for the drug before birth.

While smoking or using tobacco during pregnancy does not guarantee any of these harmful results, it is a totally avoidable risk. Why risk a baby's life before he or she even has a chance to be smoke-free?

Is Smokeless Tobacco Safer?

Some people, particularly male teenagers, know about how dangerous smoking is and have chosen to use chewing tobacco instead. Public figures and role models such as baseball players have made using chewing tobacco seem attractive. But though smoking is by far the most harmful way to use tobacco, using smokeless tobacco can be risky in other ways.

People who use chewing tobacco and snuff absorb nicotine and other chemicals through the mucous membranes in the mouth. It takes from 5 to 30 minutes for the nicotine in chewing tobacco to reach the brain. Chewing-tobacco users risk developing **tumors** (abnormal tissue growths) in the mouth or throat, where the tobacco and tobacco juice are in contact with the mucous membranes. Tobacco chewers may also develop disfiguring mouth diseases. And because smokeless tobacco often contains higher levels of nicotine than cigarettes, using these products can be even more addictive than smoking.

Now that you know about all the severe health risks of tobacco and nicotine, you may wonder why anyone would even consider using tobacco. In the next chapter, we'll discuss some of the reasons people turn to drugs like nicotine.

Did you know that the tip of a lit cigarette reaches about 2,000 degrees Fahrenheit? Both the smoker and others nearby inhale the "exhaust" from this tiny blast furnace.

4

WHY DO PEOPLE USE TOBACCO?

Until the 1970s, scientists did not study smoking as a behavior. Instead, they focused on the health effects of smoking, and they studied ways to help people quit. But more recent research on how and why people smoke, and how nicotine affects the human body, has led to new ideas about how to help people quit. Today, we also have new information about how nicotine affects the brain and other important organs.

Addiction

Nicotine has a number of effects on the brain. Perhaps the most important is that this drug can actually change the way the brain functions. Addictive drugs affect the brain by tricking it into "unlocking" certain areas on the surface of **neurons** (nerve cells of the brain). These areas are called **receptor sites**. They connect the brain's cells to other parts of the body, such as muscles and organs. Nicotine's effects on the body are complex because the drug affects many different receptor sites.

Physical dependence on drugs like nicotine occurs when a user's brain cells have adapted to function in the presence of the drug. As a result, they cannot function normally without it. When users stop taking the drug, they suffer from withdrawal. Some drugs—for example, opiates like heroin—produce life-threatening withdrawal symptoms. Other drugs, such as nicotine, produce unpleasant symptoms that are difficult and uncomfortable but do not threaten the user's life.

Smoking Behavior

One of the reasons few researchers thought of studying tobacco use in the first half of the 20th century was that smoking was considered a normal, voluntary behavior. There seemed to be no reason to study "normal" behavior. We now know that nicotine is highly addictive: although people consciously choose to start smoking or using tobacco, their bodies eventually require the drug to function normally.

Political and economic considerations also played a role in preventing scientists and researchers from studying smoking as a behavior. Because governments and tobacco companies subsidize tobacco growers, the farmers' production output becomes important to local and state economies. In addition, in the United States, the federal government has earned billions of dollars from taxes on tobacco products. Political figures and parties also receive money from tobacco companies and are pressured by tobacco lobbyists not to limit tobacco production. Even some community organizations receive huge donations from tobacco companies, a fact that makes them less likely to oppose "Big Tobacco," as the powerful industry is sometimes called.

Other factors prevented the study of smoking behavior as well. It was difficult to know which aspect of smoking behavior to study, and how to measure such aspects as when smokers decide to have a cigarette, which brand they smoke, how deeply they inhale, the dose levels of nicotine, and so on.

In an effort to study these variables, scientists developed "smoking machines" that measured how much of a given chemical was in the smoke, and machines that could keep track of how many cigarettes a smoker used in a certain period of time. These machines helped bring about several important discoveries. One is that smokers automatically but unconsciously regulate how much nicotine they take in. Their bodies are so accustomed to a certain amount of nicotine that their behavior changes slightly when they are not receiving the usual amount. This is called "compensation" or "dose regulation." As a result, scientists believe that smokers who try to decrease their dependence by smoking cigarettes that contain low amounts of tar and nicotine are likely to fail. To maintain their regular dose, they will simply smoke more low-tar and low-nicotine cigarettes, or they will inhale the smoke from them more deeply.

Several studies in the 1980s also showed that tobacco

abusers unconsciously take in the amount of nicotine their body is accustomed to *regardless* of the amount in their brand of cigarettes. In other words, smokers not only adjust to the amount of smoke and carbon monoxide in their systems; they also smoke in a way that will deliver the amount of nicotine their addicted brains need to feel normal.

Nicotine and Other Drugs

Scientists have also discovered that using other drugs while smoking affects the smoker's behavior. For example, most smokers light more cigarettes and inhale more deeply when they're drinking alcohol than when they're not drinking. This behavior was long thought to be similar to the behavior known as "social drinking," in which people who drink alcohol around other drinkers tend to drink more themselves. But later studies found that people smoke more cigarettes while drinking because of the changes that occur in the body when alcohol is ingested. Other drugs, such as cocaine, sedatives, and narcotics, also cause smokers who already use these drugs to increase their use.

Tobacco is known as a gateway drug, meaning that a person who uses it is much more likely to move on to abusing other drugs, including marijuana, cocaine, and other illegal drugs. According to the National Center on Addiction and Substance Abuse at Columbia University, a 12- to 17-year-old who smokes cigarettes is 19 times more likely to use cocaine than one who does not smoke.

Some studies of smoking behavior found that certain

Nicotine is a "gateway" drug, meaning that its use often leads to other kinds of drug use. This chart shows the percentage of 12- to 17-year-old smokers who also use illegal drugs or alcohol, compared to the percentage of nonsmoking kids ages 12 to 17 who use illegal drugs or alcohol. In every category, kids who smoke cigarettes are far more likely to use other drugs than kids who don't smoke.

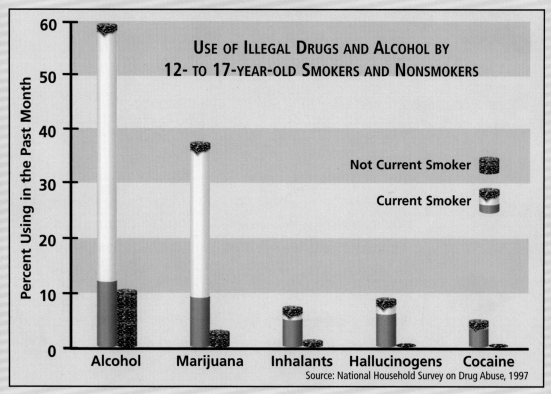

USE OF ILLEGAL DRUGS AND ALCOHOL BY 12- TO 17-YEAR-OLD SMOKERS AND NONSMOKERS

Percent Using in the Past Month

Not Current Smoker

Current Smoker

Alcohol Marijuana Inhalants Hallucinogens Cocaine

Source: National Household Survey on Drug Abuse, 1997

Tobacco companies have spent millions on advertising campaigns that aim to recruit new, young smokers with gimmicks such as the "Joe Camel" figure, who offers "Camel Cash" to spend on concert tickets (above). A number of anti-smoking advocates believe that such kid-friendly characters target

drugs inhibit the effects of nicotine. For example, mecamylamine, a drug used to combat high blood pressure, also blocks the pleasurable effects of nicotine. The immediate reaction of a smoker to this effect is to increase smoking. But if a smoker were to take such a drug regularly, he or she might give up smoking simply because there is no pleasure in it anymore. Another drug, bupropion, marketed as Wellbutrin to combat depression, has also been found to reduce nicotine cravings and

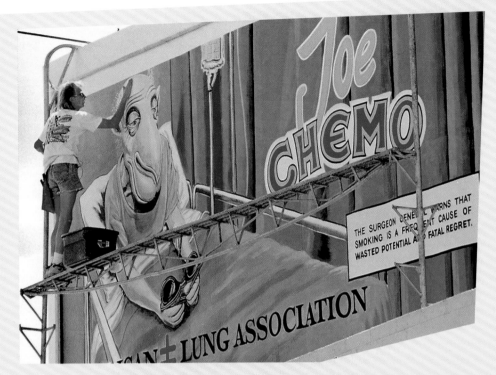

THE SURGEON GENERAL WARNS THAT SMOKING IS A FREQUENT CAUSE OF WASTED POTENTIAL AND FATAL REGRET.

children who are younger than the legal smoking age. The American Lung Association decided to fight back in 1997 by posting an ad on a billboard in Colorado (above) that pictures "Joe Chemo" (chemotherapy is a type of cancer treatment) and a far different kind of surgeon general's warning.

thus to help smokers quit. As an aid to stop smoking, this drug is marketed under another trade name, Zyban.

Are There Any Benefits to Using Tobacco?

Nicotine affects the **hormone** levels of the body by changing how much of certain brain chemicals called neurotransmitters are released. Two very important neurotransmitters are **norepinephrine**, which helps to prepare the mind and body for emergencies by widening breathing tubes and making the heart beat faster, and **dopamine**, which affects the part of the brain that controls feelings of pleasure.

Nicotine may also have some effect on weight control. It does this in different ways. One way is that it suppresses a person's appetite, particularly for sweets. Another is that it increases metabolism. Of course, a much healthier way to lose weight is to exercise and eat the proper foods. Another way that nicotine use aids weight control is by reducing stress-induced eating; when stressed, smokers usually go for a cigarette rather than for the refrigerator. Finally, nicotine suppresses the process of digestion: food is eliminated before it can be converted to fat or muscle.

Many smokers claim that if they were to quit smoking they would gain weight. It is true that one-third of those who are former smokers gain weight, but in the majority of these people, the weight gain is under five pounds. Maintaining your weight or losing a few pounds is hardly worth the risks of smoking.

It is abundantly clear that the health risks of tobacco use far outweigh any benefits. Tobacco is probably the only legal substance that causes disease and death when used as directed. Smoking causes over 400,000 deaths each year in the United States alone. Any health benefits from tobacco use are easily canceled out by the huge risks.

Smoking and Teens

For the most part, people use tobacco because they are addicted to nicotine and have not tried to quit, or they have found it too hard to quit. But the thousands of American children who begin smoking each day also have other reasons to do so.

Even some kids who know how harmful tobacco is still think smoking cigarettes and using tobacco are cool. They may think smoking is glamorous because they see lots of movies that portray beautiful, interesting people who smoke. It's easy to want to emulate these people, even when they use tobacco or other drugs. And cigarette advertising—billboards, magazine ads, tobacco company merchandise, and logos—is usually attractive and brightly colored. The ads make smoking look like fun. They make smokers look like individuals who value their personal rights and freedom. Some of them even make smoking look healthy. They make a dangerous drug look cool.

Kids in particular may believe that smoking makes them "rebels." They think that because they are legally prohibited from smoking or buying tobacco products, they are getting away with something when they have a cigarette. Smoking seems like a thrill. Think about this, though: if you smoke and have a parent, relative, or friend who smokes, how does this make you a rebel? You're doing the same thing that they are doing.

Maybe you've already tried cigarettes or other tobacco products. How do you quit? Maybe you're determined never to use these substances. How do you keep that promise to yourself? In the next chapter, we'll examine ways that people can quit smoking and stay tobacco-free.

Most smokers try their first cigarette between ages 11 and 14. These 10-year-olds attending an anti-tobacco rally in Illinois are already aware of the dangers of smoking. Does your school or community offer programs that help you learn about nicotine and other drugs? If not, maybe you can help start one!

5

SAYING NO AND GETTING HELP

Most smokers would like to quit, but because they are physically dependent on nicotine, they find quitting very hard to do. The physical withdrawal symptoms from nicotine last about a week, but tobacco users also develop a **psychological dependence**, which lasts much longer and is very difficult to break. A person who becomes psychologically dependent on a drug develops strong cravings to use the drug, even if he or she has no withdrawal symptoms or physical urge to do so.

One withdrawal symptom is dizziness, because the blood vessels in the brain that had been constricted by nicotine expand again when it is gone. Another symptom is increased coughing, which occurs as the lungs struggle to clear out dirt and deposits. Nicotine withdrawal symptoms also include irritability and nervousness. Millions of Americans have quit smoking without any help, but for these people the chances of starting smoking again are statistically very high.

For a long time people believed that quitting tobacco use was just a matter of willpower. Those who tried to quit and failed, it was believed, just didn't want to quit badly enough or didn't try hard enough. Now we know that nicotine is addictive and that quitting requires changing a number of habits associated with smoking or tobacco use. It's hard to change many of these habits, particularly for people who began using tobacco during adolescence or have been smoking for a long time. Some smokers even begin to feel that smoking is part of their personality—an idea that is a very powerful deterrent to quitting. But smoking is not a personality trait; it is part of a smoker's behavior. And behavior can be changed.

What If I Smoke for a While and Then Quit?

Most teens believe that smoking for a couple of years will not harm them, and very few think they will actually become lifelong nicotine addicts. Not true. The very first cigarette you smoke begins to damage your heart, lungs, brain, and other organs. With the very first puff of a cigarette, you are at a serious risk of becoming addicted. And don't forget: a "smoker" is defined as someone who smokes at least one cigarette a week. You're not "sort of smoking" if you've tried more than one cigarette—you *are* smoking.

And statistics show that if you try one cigarette, you probably won't quit after just a few. Instead, you are very likely to become a smoker. Surveys have shown that even though most high school–age smokers claim that they intend to quit within 5 years or less, many of them are still smoking 10 years later.

Research also shows that a nicotine addiction is actually stronger in those who began smoking at a young age than in those who began smoking as adults. Given the serious health risks of smoking and the great difficulty smokers have with quitting, starting to smoke with the intention of quitting is a pretty dumb move. It makes much better sense never to start.

Addiction can happen quickly—and it is much more powerful than most people realize. The phrase "once an addict, always an addict" applies to nicotine users as well as abusers of other drugs: a single cigarette can start a recovering smoker back on the road to addiction. When 85 percent of smokers say they wish they had never started, why would you even consider trying it?

In the Habit

One reason quitting smoking can be so difficult is because of the social and psychological "triggers" that make an addicted person want to smoke. For example, a smoker may grow accustomed to having a cigarette after dinner each evening not just for the nicotine, but because smoking is a routine activity that he or she associates with pleasant feelings and relaxation. Breaking that psychological connection can be extremely difficult. Many ex-smokers say that even after years of being tobacco-free, they still occasionally feel such cravings.

According to the American Lung Association, each cigarette you smoke shortens your life by 12 minutes. These teens are losing 48 minutes of their lives during this short smoke break.

Talking on the phone, reading the newspaper, or having a morning cup of coffee are other activities that some ex-smokers have said they have trouble doing without feeling a strong desire for a cigarette. Physical dependence on nicotine can be broken in the first few days or weeks after quitting, but psychological dependence is often longer-lasting.

Never Stop Quitting

For each person who finally quits smoking, there are many others who try to quit and fail. No one method works for everyone, and some people need to try a number of approaches before they find one that works for them. It's important to remember, though, that every time smokers try to quit—even if they fail—they are closer to the time when they will finally succeed.

In a book about drug use called *Buzzed*, authors Cynthia Kuhn, Scott Swartzwelder, and Wilkie Wilson describe this process. "Every person is different and every addiction is different," they write. "If trying on one's own did not work, a treatment program might. If one treatment program did not work, a different one might. Enough types of help are available that there is a good chance [that] one will work for any motivated person who wants to quit smoking." The facts back this up: 90 percent of people who stay smoke-free for one year never start smoking again.

Ways to Quit

There are many aids to quitting, including nicotine replacement therapy (nicotine gum, the **nicotine patch**, or a nicotine nasal spray), support groups, drugs such as Zyban, or nontraditional treatments like **acupuncture** and hypnosis. Many people who quit smoking are able to do so on their own, some without any aids or therapy at all or without tapering off cigarette use. This method is called quitting **cold turkey**.

Smoking cessation programs have had some success, but studies show that many smokers who use this method return to their old habit within six months to a year.

Nicotine chewing gum, nicotine skin patches, and a newer product—nicotine nasal spray—provide a steady but small amount of nicotine to the smoker trying to quit. However, the amount of nicotine does not come close to the amount a person gets from a cigarette. Instead, it's just enough to reduce the cravings and irritability associated with nicotine withdrawal. Nicotine gum and patches also deliver the drug slowly over time, rather than in pleasurable "jolts," to the ex-smoker's brain. And of course, the ex-smoker is free of the dangerous chemicals in cigarette smoke. Patches and gum both come in varying dosages of nicotine. A user begins with a higher dosage, then gradually switches to lower and lower dosages until he or she can stop using the gum or patch altogether.

It's important to use nicotine replacement therapy under the supervision of a health professional. It's also extremely important not to use it while smoking, because there is danger of nicotine overdose. All of these nicotine replacement aids work better when combined with a treatment program that helps the ex-smoker change behavioral triggers. Counseling and stress reduction are also important ways of helping ex-smokers stay off nicotine.

Some people report dizziness, headaches, upset stomach, weakness, vivid dreams, and other mild effects from using nicotine replacement products. But their use can greatly reduce the side effects of nicotine withdrawal. Most people using nicotine replacement probably would prefer these side effects over the powerful withdrawal symptoms they would otherwise experience.

It helps most smokers to know that they're not alone in their struggle to quit. The American Cancer Society (ACS) sponsors an annual daylong event called the Great American Smokeout during which all smokers are encouraged to quit for that day—or longer. The ACS reports that an average of 17 million people quit on each Smokeout day, and that 4 million of them are still smoke-free three months later.

What If It's Too Late to Quit?

It's *never* too late to quit. Just as the amount of nicotine in the blood dramatically decreases within 20 minutes after a smoker finishes a cigarette, the health benefits of quitting begin immediately. The longer a person smokes or uses tobacco, the greater the risk of serious health complications and premature death. But the longer a person stays off nicotine, the better the chances are for recovery and reversal of much of the damage done by smoking. The American Cancer Society lists some of the immediate and long-term health benefits of quitting smoking:

- After 20 minutes, blood pressure drops to normal.
- After eight hours, the carbon monoxide level in the blood drops to normal.
- After 48 hours, nerve endings start regrowing and the senses of smell and taste are enhanced.
- In one to nine months, coughing, sinus congestion, fatigue, and shortness of breath decrease and **cilia**

(tiny, hair-like cells that move continually to clean air that is breathed in) regrow in the lungs.

- After five years, the chance of dying from lung cancer decreases by almost half.
- After 15 years, the risk of heart disease is equal to that of a nonsmoker, and the risk of dying from lung cancer is only slightly higher than that of a nonsmoker.

It is important to note that the extent to which these risks fall depends on the total amount the person smoked, the age the person started smoking, and the amount of inhalation.

"But what if I can't quit?" you may ask. You can! It's not impossible; millions of people have done it. The appendix in the back of this book contains information about where to get help to quit smoking and where to find out more about nicotine, tobacco, and your health.

Don't Most People Smoke?

No! The percentage of American adults who smoke has dropped from 42 percent in 1965 to 25 percent in 1993. And although many young people believe that "everyone" smokes, it's just not true. In fact, surveys show that most teens disapprove of smoking and would rather not hang around with smokers.

Is Someone You Know Using Tobacco?

It's usually easier to tell if a friend or relative is using tobacco than if he or she is using other kinds of drugs. A

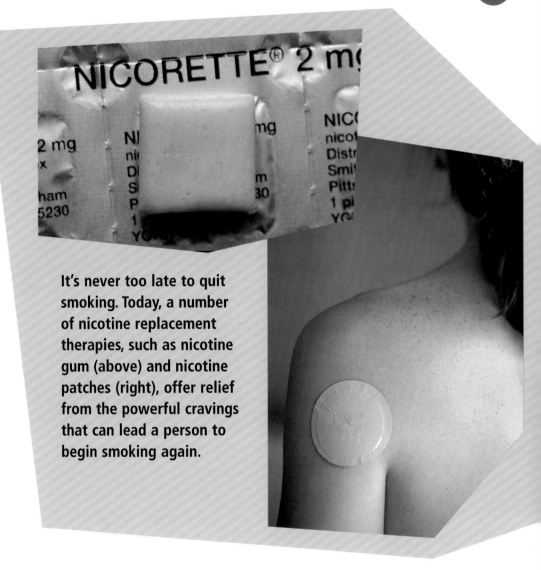

It's never too late to quit smoking. Today, a number of nicotine replacement therapies, such as nicotine gum (above) and nicotine patches (right), offer relief from the powerful cravings that can lead a person to begin smoking again.

person who smokes will (obviously) smell like smoke. The odor clings to clothing, hair, fingers, and breath even when a person smokes outside. There may also be ashes or burn marks in clothing.

People who use chewing tobacco usually have stains on teeth or may have bits of tobacco leaf in their mouths. Spit tobacco also requires the user to do just that—spit!

Opening the Gateway

Don't forget that tobacco, along with alcohol and marijuana, is a gateway drug. Read the following facts, collected by the National Center on Addiction and Substance Abuse at Columbia University, about the risk of drinkers, marijuana smokers, and cigarette smokers developing a cocaine habit. Then ask yourself: Am I willing to take that risk?

- A 12- to 17-year-old who smokes cigarettes is 19 times more likely to use cocaine than one who does not smoke.
- An adolescent who drinks alcohol is 50 times more likely to use cocaine than one who does not drink.
- A 12- to 17-year-old who smokes pot is 85 times more likely to use cocaine than one who does not use pot.
- Adolescents who drink and smoke pot and cigarettes are 266 times more likely to use cocaine than those who don't use any of these drugs.
- The earlier in life people use alcohol, tobacco, and marijuana, the more likely they are to go on to harder drugs. Sixty percent of kids who begin smoking pot before the age of 15 will eventually use cocaine.

How Can I Say No?

Most smokers start smoking between the ages of 11 and 14. Why? It can be hard to resist harmful activities like drinking alcohol or smoking tobacco or marijuana when it seems that everyone does it. Maybe you think that tobacco, alcohol, or other drugs can help you fit in, feel more relaxed, or have more fun. But now that you know what tobacco does to you—and what a lifetime of addiction means—you can find ways to avoid doing what you know is bad for you.

There are some ways you can protect yourself from peer pressure to do something harmful. Avoid parties where you know there will be alcohol or other drugs. Seek out friends who don't use these substances and stay away from people who do. Get involved in your community by joining clubs or local groups with activities that interest you, and you'll be too busy to use drugs or alcohol. You'll have a lot more fun, stay healthy, and live longer. And you'll feel better about yourself because you stuck to your decision not to use tobacco and didn't give in to what others may have wanted you to do.

Remember, the majority of Americans do not smoke. The majority of teens do not smoke. Despite what you may hear, everybody is *not* doing it. And if you want to stay healthy and strong, you won't either.

acupuncture—a treatment for curing disease or relieving pain that originated in China, in which needles are used to pierce the skin at specific areas of the body, called pressure points.

addiction—a condition of some drug users that is caused by repeated drug use. An addicted user becomes physically dependent on the drug and continues to take it, despite severe negative consequences. A drug user's body develops a tolerance to the drug and needs increasingly large amounts of the drug to achieve the same level of "high."

asthma—a usually chronic lung ailment; main symptoms are wheezing, coughing, and difficulty breathing. Smoking can significantly worsen asthma.

bidis—flavored, unfiltered cigarettes imported from India that deliver twice the tar and seven times the nicotine as regular cigarettes.

black market—production, distribution, or sale of a product or substance that violates official regulations.

blood pressure—pressure of the blood against the walls of the arteries. Smoking can raise a person's blood pressure, making the heart work harder.

bronchitis—an illness caused by the infection and swelling of the lining of the bronchial tubes (the two main branches of the trachea that carry air to the lungs). Symptoms include a severe cough and a hoarse voice.

bubonic plague—also called "Black Death," a contagious and deadly disease that causes the growth of lumps, or "buboes," on the body. Epidemics of this disease first struck Europe during the 14th century and periodically recurred until about 1800.

cancer—a disease involving abnormal cells that do not stop growing.

Cancer can spread from where it begins in the body and destroy healthy tissues and organs. Smoking causes cancer.

carbon monoxide—a toxic gas with no color or smell. Carbon monoxide is emitted from burning cigarettes and other substances.

carcinogenic—causing or contributing to the growth of cancer.

chewing tobacco—tobacco in the form of loose, twisted leaves that are held in the mouth and chewed. The product is usually packaged loosely in pouches, or in "plugs" or bricks.

cilia—tiny, hairlike cells that line the bronchi and move continually to clean the air that is breathed.

cocaine—a powerful stimulant made from the leaves of the coca plant and usually sold as a white powder. Cocaine is highly addictive.

cold turkey—a phrase used to describe quitting a substance or habit, such as smoking, without tapering off or using additional aids.

curing—preparing or preserving something by using a special process. For example, tobacco is cured by drying the leaves to be made into cigarettes, cigars, chewing tobacco, pipe tobacco, or snuff.

dip—finely cut, ground, or powdered tobacco. Dried dip, or snuff, is usually inhaled through the nose; moist snuff, which is more common in the United States, is placed in the mouth and held there (not chewed).

dopamine—a neurotransmitter in the brain. Dopamine is released by neurons in the limbic system, a part of the brain that controls feelings of pleasure.

emphysema—a disease that prevents the lungs from expanding and contracting normally. Cigarette smoking has been linked to emphysema.

ETS—environmental tobacco smoke, also called passive smoking; a term used to describe tobacco smoke that is breathed in from the environment when someone nearby is smoking. ETS includes secondhand smoke and sidestream smoke.

gateway drug—a drug whose use may lead to use of stronger drugs such as cocaine and heroin. Tobacco is considered a gateway drug.

hemoglobin—a substance in red blood cells that bonds with and carries oxygen to the cells where it is needed. Carbon monoxide in cigarette smoke bonds more strongly with hemoglobin than oxygen does.

herba panacea—a cure-all herb or plant.

heroin—a drug made from the milky juice of the poppy plant called *Papaver somniferum*. Heroin is the common name for diacetylmorphine, one of the strongest of the opiate drugs. It is highly addictive.

hormone—a substance produced by a gland in the endocrine system and carried by the blood to body organs and tissue. Hormones regulate some body functions and control growth.

hypothalamus—the gland in the brain that controls mood, appetite, blood pressure, and production of certain hormones.

lobbyists—people whose job is to influence legislators to pass laws beneficial to their cause, or not to pass laws detrimental to that cause. For example, the tobacco industry has used lobbyists to convince lawmakers not to pass bills limiting cigarette sales.

marijuana—a psychoactive drug derived from the *Cannabis sativa* plant that is smoked or eaten for its initial effect of euphoria or relaxation.

neuron—a nerve cell in the brain.

nicotine—the highly addictive substance found in the tobacco plant and in all tobacco products.

nicotine gum—a special gum containing nicotine, which is used to help reduce withdrawal symptoms in people who are quitting tobacco use.

nicotine patch—an adhesive skin patch containing a small amount of nicotine. The nicotine is absorbed into the body through the skin, thus helping to reduce withdrawal symptoms in people who are quitting tobacco use.

norepinephrine—a neurotransmitter in the brain. Norepinephrine helps to prepare the mind and body for emergencies by widening breathing tubes and making the heart beat faster.

oral cancer—cancer of the mouth, lips, gums, tongue, larynx (voice box), and esophagus (the tube that connects the mouth to the stomach). Tobacco use has been linked with oral cancer.

passive smoking—a term used to describe the involuntary inhaling of tobacco smoke. People who are around a smoker breathe in tobacco smoke whether or not they themselves are smoking.

peer pressure—words or actions by a friend, a sibling, or someone else of your own age group that make you feel as though you have to act like them to fit in with the group.

pesticides—chemicals that are used to kill harmful pests, such as insects or rodents.

physical dependence—addiction; the state in which a drug user's body chemistry has adapted to require regular doses of a drug to function normally. Stopping the drug causes withdrawal symptoms. Nicotine causes severe physical dependence.

placenta—an organ that grows in a pregnant woman's uterus that connects to the fetus to provide nutrients and oxygen. The placenta is expelled after the baby is born.

psychological dependence—the state of addiction in which certain brain changes create strong cravings to use the drug, even if the user has no withdrawal symptoms or physical urge to do so. Nicotine causes psychological dependence.

receptor site—a special area of a cell that combines with a chemical substance to alter the cell's function.

secondhand smoke—tobacco smoke that is exhaled by smokers and inhaled by people nearby.

sidestream smoke—tobacco smoke that is emitted from the lighted end of a cigarette or cigar or from a lighted pipe.

snuff—a preparation of dry or moist powdered tobacco that is inhaled through the nose.

spit tobacco—another name for dip, snuff, or chewing tobacco.

stimulant—a substance that increases or speeds up the functions and activities of the body. Examples of stimulants are nicotine, caffeine, cocaine, amphetamines, and methamphetamine.

subsidize—to aid or promote by paying a sum of money. For example, tobacco companies may subsidize community groups to build feelings of goodwill toward their industry; the U.S. federal government subsidizes farmers to help them stay in business even when they have a bad year.

tar—a residue present in smoke from burning tobacco products that can adhere to the lining of the lungs and cause health problems.

tolerance—a condition in which a drug user requires increasing amounts of the drug to achieve the same level of intoxication previously obtained by using smaller amounts.

tumor—an abnormal growth of tissue that may or may not be cancerous.

withdrawal—the symptoms that occur when a person who is physically dependent on a drug stops taking the drug.

BIBLIOGRAPHY

Cohen, Philip. *Tobacco*. Austin: Steck-Vaughn, 1992.

Haughton, Emma. *A Right to Smoke?* New York: Franklin Watts, 1996.

Henningfield, Jack E. *Nicotine: An Old-Fashioned Addiction*. New York: Chelsea House Publishers, 1992.

Hurwitz, Sue, and Nancy Shniderman. *Drugs and Your Friends*. New York: Rosen Publishing Group, 1992.

Hyde, Margaret. *Know About Smoking*. New York: Walker and Co., 1995.

Kreiner, Anna. *Let's Talk About Drug Abuse*. New York: PowerKids Press, 1996.

Kuhn, Cynthia; Scott Swartzwelder; and Wilkie Wilson. *Buzzed: The Straight Facts About the Most Used and Abused Drugs from Alcohol to Ecstasy*. New York: W. W. Norton and Co., 1998.

Lang, Susan, and Beth Marks. *Teens and Tobacco: A Fatal Attraction*. New York: Twenty-First Century Books, 1996.

Monroe, Judy. *Nicotine*. Springfield, NJ: Enslow Publishers, 1995.

Myers, Arthur. *Drugs and Emotions*. New York: Rosen Publishing Group, 1996.

_____. *Drugs and Peer Pressure*. New York: Rosen Publishing Group, 1995.

Pietrusza, David. *Smoking*. San Diego: Lucent Books, 1997.

Pringle, Laurence. *Smoking: A Risky Business*. New York: Morrow Junior Books, 1996.

Sanders, Pete, and Steve Myers. *What Do You Know About Smoking?* London: Aladdin Books, 1996.

Weitzman, Elizabeth. *Let's Talk About Smoking*. New York: PowerKids Press, 1996.

FIND OUT MORE ABOUT NICOTINE, CIGARETTES, AND DRUG ABUSE

The following list includes agencies, organizations, and websites that provide information about nicotine and smoking. You can also find out where to go for help with a drug problem.

Many national organizations have local chapters listed in your phone directory. Look under "Smokers Information and Treatment Centers" or "Drug Abuse and Addiction" to find resources in your area.

Agencies and Organizations in the United States

Action on Smoking and Health
2013 H Street, N.W.
Washington, DC 20006
202-659-4310

American Cancer Society
1599 Clifton Road, N.E.
Atlanta, GA 30329
404-320-3333 or 800-ACS-2345 (227-2345)

American Council for Drug Education
164 West 74th Street
New York, NY 10023
212-758-8060 or 800-488-DRUG (3784)
http://www.acde.org/
wlittlefield@phoenixhouse.org

American Heart Association
7320 Greenville Avenue
Dallas, TX 75231

American Lung Association
1740 Broadway
New York, NY 10019-4374
800-LUNG-USA (586-4872)
http://www.lungusa.org/

Center for Substance Abuse Treatment
Information and Treatment Referral Hotline
11426-28 Rockville Pike, Suite 410
Rockville, MD 20852
800-662-HELP (4357)

Coalition on Smoking or Health
1150 Connecticut Avenue, N.W.
Suite 820
Washington, DC 20036
202-452-1184

**Group Against Smokers'
Pollution (GASP)**
P.O. Box 632
College Park, MD 20741-0632
301-459-4791

Just Say No International
2000 Franklin Street, Suite 400
Oakland, CA 94612
800-258-2766

National Cancer Institute
Building 31, Room 10A24
Bethesda, MD 20892
800-40-CANCER (402-2623)

**National Center
for Health Education**
72 Spring Street, Suite 208
New York, NY 10012-4019
212-334-9470

**National Center on Addiction
and Substance Abuse at
Columbia University**
152 West 57th Street
New York, NY 10019-3310
212-841-5200 or 212-956-8020
http://www.casacolumbia.org/home.htm

**National Clearinghouse
for Alcohol and Drug
Information (NCADI)**
P.O. Box 2345
Rockville, MD 20847-2345
800-729-6686
800-487-4889 TDD
800-HI-WALLY (449-2559, Children's Line)
http://www.health.org/

**National Health
Information Center**
P.O. Box 1133
Washington, DC 20013-1133
800-336-4797

Nicotine Anonymous
P.O. Box 591777
San Francisco, CA 94159-1777
415-750-0328

**Parents' Resource Institute
for Education (PRIDE)**
3610 DeKalb Technology Parkway, Suite 105
Atlanta, GA 30340
770-458-9900
http://www.prideusa.org/

Shalom, Inc.
311 South Juniper Street
Room 900
Philadelphia, PA 19107
215-546-3470

**Stop Teenage Addiction
to Tobacco (STAT)**
511 East Columbus Ave.
Springfield, MA 01105
413-732-7828

Addiction Research Foundation (ARF)
33 Russell Street
Toronto, Ontario M5S 2S1
416-595-6100
800-463-6273 in Ontario

Addictions Foundation of Manitoba
1031 Portage Avenue
Winnipeg, Manitoba R3G 0R8
204-944-6277
http://www.mbnet.mb.ca/crm/health/afm.html

British Columbia Prevention Resource Centre
96 East Broadway, Suite 211
Vancouver, British Columbia V5T 1V6
604-874-8452
800-663-1880 in British Columbia

Canadian Cancer Society
33 Russell Street
Toronto, Ontario M5S 2S1

Canadian Centre on Substance Abuse
75 Albert Street, Suite 300
Ottawa, Ontario K1P 5E7
613-235-4048
http://www.ccsa.ca/

Canadian Council on Tobacco Control
http://www.cctc.ca/

Canadian Heart Foundation
1 Nicholas Street, Suite 1200
Ottawa, Ontario K1N7-B7

Canadian Lung Association
75 Albert Street, Suite 908
Ottawa, Ontario K1P 5E7
http://www.lung.ca/

Office of Tobacco Reduction Programs, Health Canada
http://www.hc-sc.gc.ca/hppb/tobaccoreduction/

Ontario Healthy Communities Central Office
180 Dundas Street West, Suite 1900
Toronto, Ontario M5G 1Z8
416-408-4841
http://www.opc.on.ca/ohcc/

Quit4Life
http://www.quit4life.com/html/splash.html

Saskatchewan Health Resource Centre
T.C. Douglas Building
3475 Albert Street
Regina, Saskatchewan S4S 6X6
306-787-3090

Websites

Avery Smartcat's Facts & Research on Children Facing Drugs
http://www.averysmartcat.com/druginfo.htm

Centers for Disease Control and Prevention (CDC)
http://www.cdc.gov/

Internet Public Library Teen Division
http://www.ipl.org/cgi-bin/teen/

Join Together Online
http://www.jointogether.org/sa/

National Institute on Drug Abuse (NIDA)
http://www.nida.nih.gov

No Smoke Cafe
http://www.clever.net/chrisco/nosmoke/cafe.html

Partnership for a Drug-Free America
http://www.drugfreeamerica.org/

Reality Check
http://www.health.org/reality/

Substance Abuse and Mental Health Services Administration (SAMHSA)
http://www.samhsa.gov

TalkZone: Marion Foundation Teen Services
http://www.talkzone.org

Tobacco Facts
http://www.tobaccofacts.org

United Nations International Drug Control Program
http://www.undcp.or.at/

U.S. Department of Education Safe and Drug-Free Schools Program
http://inet.ed.gov/offices/OESE/SDFS

U.S. Department of Justice Kids' Page
http://www.usdoj.gov/kidspage/

Virtual Clearinghouse on Alcohol, Tobacco and Other Drugs
http://www.atod.org/

INDEX

PICTURE CREDITS

page
6: Courtesy Office of National
    Drug Control Policy, the White
    House
12: PhotoDisc Vol. 25 #25330
15: Blair Seitz/Photo Researchers,
    Inc.
22: AP/Wide World Photos
25: Werner Forman/Art Resource,
    NY
26: AP/Wide World Photos
29: Van Bucher/Photo
    Researchers, Inc.
32: AP/Wide World Photos
36: Oscar Burriel/Latin Stock/
    Science Photo Library/Photo
    Researchers, Inc.

41: Martin M. Rotker/Science
    Source/Photo Researchers, Inc.
42: © Conor Caffrey/SPL/Photo
    Researchers, Inc.
46: PhotoDisc Vol. 25 #25329
51: (top) Michael P. Gadomski/
    Photo Researchers, Inc.; (bot-
    tom) illustration by Keith Trego
52: AP/Wide World Photos
53: AP/Wide World Photos
56: AP/Wide World Photos
60: AP/Wide World Photos
65: (top) Will & Deni McIntyre/
    Photo Researchers, Inc.;
    (bottom) Scott Camazine/Photo
    Researchers, Inc.

GINA DE ANGELIS is a former smoker who, like most smokers, wishes she had never started. She holds a B.A. from Marlboro College and an M.A. from the University of Mississippi. She is a freelance writer living in southern Virginia. This is her sixth book for Chelsea House.

BARRY R. McCAFFREY is director of the Office of National Drug Control Policy (ONDCP) at the White House and a member of President Bill Clinton's cabinet. Before taking this job, General McCaffrey was an officer in the U.S. Army. He led the famous "left hook" maneuver of Operation Desert Storm that helped the United States win the Persian Gulf War.

STEVEN L. JAFFE, M.D., received his psychiatry training at Harvard University and the Massachusetts Mental Health Center and his child psychiatry training at Emory University. He has been editor of the *Newsletter of the American Academy of Child and Adolescent Psychiatry* and chairman of the Continuing Education Committee of the Georgia Psychiatric Physicians' Association. Dr. Jaffe is professor of child and adolescent psychiatry at Emory University. He is also clinical professor of psychiatry at Morehouse School of Medicine, and the director of Adolescent Substance Abuse Programs at Charter Peachford Hospital in Atlanta, Georgia.